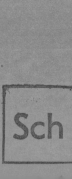

COUNTRIES IN OUR WORLD

BRAZIL

Edward Parker

FRANKLIN WATTS
LONDON•SYDNEY

First published in 2009 by
Franklin Watts
338 Euston Road
London NW1 3BH

Franklin Watts Australia
Level 17/207 Kent Street
Sydney NSW 2000

W Produced for Franklin Watts by
White-Thomson Publishing Ltd
+44 (0) 845 362 8240
www.wtpub.co.uk

Series consultant: Rob Bowden
Editor: Sonya Newland
Designer: Alix Wood
Picture researcher: Amy Sparks

A CIP catalogue record for this book is available from
the British Library.

Dewey Classification: 918.1

ISBN 978 0 7496 8846 2

Printed in Malaysia

Franklin Watts is a division of Hachette
Children's Books, an Hachette UK company.

www.hachette.co.uk

Picture Credits
Corbis: Cover (Gavin Hellier/Robert Harding World
Imagery), 7 (Ben Radford), 9 (Sergio Pitamitz), 14
(Marc Lecureuil), 22 (Paulo Fridman), 24 (Paulo
Fridman), 27 (Robert Maass), 28 (Carlos Cazalis);
Dreamstime: 8 (Tony1), 18 (Mortenelm); **iStock:** 4,
10, 20; **Edward Parker:** 13, 29; **Photoshot:** 15 (WpN),
25 (WpN); **Shutterstock:** 1 (Celso Pupo), 16 (Pres
Panatoyov), 17 (David Davis), 19 (Rafael Martin-
Gaitero), 21 (Vinicius Tupinamba), 23 (Celso Pupo), 26
(Franck Camhi); **White-Thomson Publishing:** 6, 11, 12.

Contents

Introducing Brazil

Brazil is the fifth largest country in the world. It is bigger than Europe, almost 55 times the size of the UK and has borders with all South American countries except Ecuador and Chile. The largest river in the world, the Amazon, runs through Brazil, and it also has the largest area of unbroken rainforest on the planet.

▼ The statue of Christ the Redeemer towers above Rio de Janeiro, the second largest city in Brazil. The statue has been named one of the New Seven Wonders of the World.

Brazil has international land borders with 10 of the other 12 South American countries – Argentina, Bolivia, Colombia, French Guiana, Guyana, Paraguay, Peru, Suriname, Uruguay and Venezuela.

A global influence for 500 years

Brazil has had global connections ever since the Portuguese explorer Pedro Cabral arrived there in 1500. The Portuguese cut down Brazil's rare trees to extract a dye from the wood, and dug for minerals such as gold and diamonds. Soon, plantations were established to grow crops such as sugar and coffee, and slaves were brought from West Africa to provide labour. The plantations made the Portuguese fabulously wealthy and influenced the development of the European economy.

The rubber boom

Brazil gained independence in 1822, and the Brazilian people began to enjoy their country's wealth for themselves, particularly at the end of the nineteenth century during the 'rubber boom'. The demand for rubber for vehicle tyres was so great that the Amazonian city of Manaus briefly became richer than New York. However, soon after this, the Brazilian economy began to decline. Later, the coffee boom encouraged people from countries such as Italy and Japan to move to Brazil to work.

▲ *Brazil has nearly one quarter of all the fresh water on Earth flowing through it, which gives it great potential for hydroelectricity.*

The BRIC countries

In the 1950s, Brazil began a massive development programme. The Brazilian government borrowed money from wealthy countries to build factories, roads, ports and power stations. Today, it is one of the four most important developing nations in the world; these countries are known together as BRIC, which stands for Brazil, Russia, India and China. They have a major influence on the world because between them these countries have huge natural resources and more than a third of the world's workforce. As the BRIC countries develop, they are changing the global economy.

Natural resources

Brazil has a huge wealth of natural resources, including some of the world's largest deposits of iron ore, bauxite (used to make aluminium), diamonds and gold. Production of many of these resources, especially gold, declined in the 1990s, as restrictions on mining in the Amazon were introduced. Recently, though, investment in mining has increased again. Brazil is also the world's largest producer of sugar, oranges and beef. However, the country's development has led to the destruction of large areas of rainforest, contributing to global climate change, which is now affecting the whole planet.

BASIC DATA

Official name: Federal Republic of Brazil

Capital: Brasilia

Size: 8,511,965 sq km (3,286,488 sq miles)

Population: 196,342,592

Currency: Real

FAMOUS BRAZILIAN

Pelé
(b. 1940)

Pelé is one of the most famous living Brazilians. He starred in the 1970 and 1974 football World Cup finals, where his brilliance made him a household name around the world. Since retiring from football, he has worked to raise awareness of and find solutions to poverty in Brazil.

Brazil around the world

Brazilian culture has spread around the world and Brazilian communities can be found in major cities from London to New York. Brazilian art, music, literature and architecture are now famous throughout the world. Brazil is famous for introducing the rest of the world to the samba dance, bossa nova music and what many people consider to be the most stylish way of playing football.

◀ *Brazilian football star Kaká is tackled by England player David Beckham. Kaká was named FIFA World Player of the Year in 2007.*

South-east

The South-east region covers around 10 per cent of Brazil. It is an area of rolling hills with an average altitude of 700 m (2,297 ft) above sea level. This area receives high rainfall and the land is good for large-scale farming. The South-east region has metal and mineral deposits, as well as Brazil's most important oil fields. Industry and services are also important to the economy here. The South-east borders the Atlantic Ocean, and several of Brazil's main cities are located along the coast, including Rio de Janeiro and São Paulo.

South

The South region has gently rolling hills in some areas, which give way to rugged mountains and forested valleys. Some parts of the South are very similar to the Alpine areas of Germany and Italy. The European-style landscape has attracted Italian and German immigrants to cultivate vineyards and set up Brazil's wine industry here. The landscape is well suited to other types of European-style agriculture, including dairy farming to produce milk for the food-processing industry.

▼ *Rio de Janeiro, with its famous natural landmark Sugar Loaf Mountain, is situated on the south-east coast of Brazil.*

Brazil's climate

Brazil's climate is varied. The Amazon region has a very even climate. It is hot and wet all year round, with daytime temperatures averaging 26°C (79°F) and with an annual rainfall of 1,500 to 2,000 mm (59 to 79 in). Most of the North-east coast has a warm, tropical climate, with a slightly cooler wet season between May and August and a hot, dry season between September and April. The Brazilian highlands and plateaus of the South-east and Centre-west have distinct seasons, with cool, wet winters and hot, dry summers. The very south of the country experiences four seasons similar to those in northern Italy.

▲ *Caiman alligators in the Pantanal. This is the largest wetland area in the world – during the rainy season, most of it is underwater.*

THE HOME OF...

The Pantanal

The Pantanal is a vast wetland, which becomes one huge lake the size of France during the wet season. The main farming activity in the region is cattle ranching, and the area is important for waterfowl such as scarlet ibis and cormorant. There are also large numbers of caimans, capybara (a giant rodent), marsh deer, jaguars and giant anteaters.

A young population

Brazil's population has grown rapidly over the last 50 years, and it now accounts for nearly half of the entire population of South America. Although the rate of growth has slowed in the past 10 years, Brazil's population is still growing by nearly two million people every year. The Brazilian population is very young compared to countries such as the USA, Japan or Germany – more than a quarter of Brazilians are under 14 years old. This may cause problems, because schools must be built to educate them and jobs must be found as they grow older.

GOING GLOBAL

There are thought to be between 130,000 and 160,000 Brazilians living in London. These people have taken their culture with them, and as a result there are numerous samba clubs there, and even *churrascarias*, a type of barbecue restaurant popular in Brazil.

▼ *A Brazilian carnival is celebrated on the streets of Islington, North London. The English capital has a large Brazilian population.*

Population density

In 2000, the population density of Brazil was 22 people per sq km (57 people per sq mile). However, there are huge differences in population density around the country. For example, 90 per cent of Brazilians live within 100 km (62 miles) of the Atlantic coast. São Paulo has a population density of over 3,650 people per sq km (9,495 people per sq mile), whereas in the Amazon region it can be as low as two people per sq km (five people per sq mile).

Moving to the cities

Fifty years ago, more than two-thirds of people in Brazil lived in the countryside. Today, more than 80 per cent live in towns or cities, having moved in search of work and better opportunities. There is a big divide between rich and poor in Brazil, and most of the big cities have slums known as *favelas*, where millions of people live in very poor conditions. Thousands of Brazilians have also left the country in the last 50 years, providing young workers in countries with ageing populations such as the UK and the USA.

▶ *People come to the cities to find work, but often cannot afford housing there, so instead they settle in slums called* favelas *that spring up on the outskirts of the cities.*

PLACE IN THE WORLD

Population: **196,342,592**

Percentage of world total: **2.9%**

World ranking: **5th**

Family life

Brazilian family life has changed over the last half a century. Fifty years ago, the majority of Brazilian people lived in the countryside, often with – or close to – several generations of their family. Today the majority of Brazilians live in cities. Millions have moved there in search of work, often leaving their families behind in rural areas. Women make up an increasing number of workers and there are also more single-parent families than ever before.

THE HOME OF...

Brazil nuts

All Brazil nuts are still harvested from wild trees that are among the largest that grow in the Amazon rainforest. None of the nuts that are transported from Brazil and other South American countries are grown on plantations. Each Brazil nut we eat has been cracked by hand.

Changing diet

Food is an important part of the Brazilian culture, but feeding more than 196 million people is a major challenge. Beans, rice, coffee and manioc (a plant with an edible root) are the staple foods for millions of Brazilians. There are many regional variations, with African-style food popular in the North-east region and European-style cuisine, such as cheese and wine, in the south. Many Brazilian foods are popular around the world, including Brazil nuts and acai juice. However, fast foods such as burgers and processed foods are also becoming increasingly popular.

◀ *Fruit juice made from acai berries, which are grown in the Amazon region of Brazil, has become popular all over the world because people believe it has energy-boosting properties.*

Education

Education is free for all children up until the age of 14. However, many children do not complete their education as they may have to work or help their parents look after younger children. It is also free to attend university, but the majority of university students still come from private schools.

Freedom to choose religion

Brazil has the second largest number of Christians in the world after the USA. The largest religious group is Roman Catholic, although Protestants are a fast-growing group, representing around one-fifth of the population. The Brazilian constitution states that people have the right to follow a religion of their choosing. African Brazilians follow several religions, including Candomblé.

IT'S A FACT!

The Candomblé religion is the best known of the African religions in Brazil, where it has more than a million followers. They believe that everyone has a god (Orixa), which guides and protects them, and followers also worship several other traditional African gods. Candomblé rituals involve dancing and drumming.

▼ *Followers of the Afro-Brazilian religion Candomblé gather by the sea to make offerings to the sea goddess Iemanjá.*

Manufacturing

Brazil is a major manufacturing nation, producing a huge range of goods, including vehicles, steel, textiles and footwear. Many foreign companies, including the US company Ford and the German company Volkswagen, run factories in Brazil, providing employment for many Brazilian people. In 2000, 14 of the 20 largest companies in Brazil were owned by foreign companies. Brazil ranks tenth in the world for car production.

Imports and exports

The rapid growth in Brazil's economy over the last 10 years is largely due to the increase in the goods and services that it exports to other countries. For example, the value of Brazil's exports nearly tripled from 2001 to 2007, from US$58 billion to US$161 billion. At the same time, imports grew by 46 per cent from US$56 billion to US$121 billion. The main goods that Brazil imports are machinery, electrical equipment and chemical products.

▼ *Workers weld car frames on an assembly line in Sao Caetano do Sul, in a factory owned by US company General Motors.*

▲ *This woman is making handbags from imitation leather – actually rubber. This is part of a scheme to make money from the rainforest without destroying it.*

IT STARTED HERE

Rubber

Without the discovery and production of rubber, the world's motor industry could have had a very different history. The Portuguese first discovered the Omagua Amazonian Indians using the latex from the rubber tree to waterproof items. By the end of the nineteenth century, rubber had become a multi-million pound global industry.

Trading partners

Brazil's largest single trading partner is the USA, which accounted for 16.1 per cent of all exports in 2007. However, when all exports to European countries are added together, it is even larger than that of the USA. Currently, Argentina accounts for 9.2 per cent of Brazilian exports, while China accounts for 6.8 per cent and Japan 3.0 per cent.

Brazil was a colony of Portugal for more than 300 years, which meant that the country was mainly run for the benefit of Portugal. This ended with Brazilian independence in 1822, but it was still many years before the country became the republic it is today.

From empire to republic

After 1822 Brazil was ruled by emperors, but in 1889 there was a military revolt and the emperor, Pedro II, stepped down. Brazil was declared a republic, but really the military controlled the country. Although there was a period of civilian rule, the army took over again in 1964 and it was not until 1985 that Brazil became a true republic.

The Brazilian government

Today, Brazil is a presidential republic like the USA. This means that the president is both head of the government and head of state. He is elected directly by the people. Brazil has 26 states, and each one elects its own local government. The National Congress has a president, a federal senate with 81 members, and a 513-seat chamber of deputies.

▼ *The National Congress of Brazil, in the capital Brasilia, was designed by world-famous Brazilian architect Oscar Niemeyer.*

▲ *Children greet a mascot at the 1992 Earth Summit (see box, below) to address global environmental problems.*

A new direction

In 2003, President Lula came to power. Almost immediately he tried to find ways to reduce the huge gap between rich and poor in Brazil. He changed Brazilian foreign policy, deciding that it was not good for Brazil to rely too much on Europe and the USA for overseas trade. Instead he began making trade agreements with other developing nations, including China, India and neighbouring South American countries.

IT STARTED HERE

The Earth Summit

The first Earth Summit was held in Rio de Janeiro in 1992. This meeting of United Nations countries was intended to work out ways to solve global environmental problems. Representatives from 172 nations attended the summit, and it influenced environmental policies all over the world.

Brazil in 2020

By 2020, Brazil's population may have reached 210 million. Compared to countries in Europe and North America, it will still have a young population and a large workforce, which will give it an economic advantage over countries with older populations. However, there is the potential for unrest because of the huge gap between rich and poor in Brazil.

Boom or bust?

Many developing nations may face economic problems because they are using up too many of their natural resources. This is unlikely to happen in Brazil because it has such large reserves of so many resources that it will be able to provide its industries with the materials they need. This may mean it has an increasing influence on the global economy.

GLOBAL LEADER

Biofuels

After World War II (1939–45), the Brazilian government decided that it wanted to reduce its imports such as oil. It developed an industry producing alcohol from sugar cane (biofuel) for cars. Today, Brazil is a world leader in biofuel production, and around 20 per cent of Brazilian vehicles run on biofuel.

◀ *This man is harvesting sugar cane, which will be used as a biofuel. This fuel is cheap to produce and less polluting than petrol or diesel.*

Deforestation and climate change

Brazil could suffer from environmental disaster if some of the major problems are not addressed. Deforestation in the Amazon is causing changes in weather patterns in Brazil and across the world. A change in temperature or rainfall in the large agricultural areas could be disastrous for crops. Also, some cities are already using more water than is locally available. However, Brazil has huge potential for producing renewable energy such as hydroelectric power, solar power and biofuel.

 Limiting deforestation in the rainforests, while still developing its economy, is the most pressing problem Brazil faces in the near future.

IT'S A FACT!

Brazil is already the tenth largest economy in the world. If it continues to grow at the same rate as it has for the past 10 years, it will probably overtake Spain and Italy by 2020, and possibly even France and the UK.

Glossary

biofuel a fuel usually made from a plant material, such as wheat for ethanol.

Candomblé a religion practised in Brazil that has African origins.

Capoeira a type of slow-motion dancing and fighting developed by African slaves in Brazil.

churrascaria a type of barbecue restaurant that originated in Brazil but is now popular all over the world.

constitution the agreed general principles of a formal organization such as a national government.

drainage basin an area of land that contributes water to a stream or river.

economy the financial system of a country or region, including how much money is made from the production and sale of goods and services.

export to send or transport products, materials or services abroad for sale or trade.

extinction the dying out of a particular species of plant or animal.

favelas a Brazilian word for slums or shanty towns, which are often found on the outskirts of the big cities.

global warming the gradual rise in temperatures on the surface of the Earth caused by changes in the amount of greenhouse gases in the atmosphere.

greenhouse gas any of several gases that trap warmth in the atmosphere, which can contribute to global warming if too much is generated on Earth.

import to bring in goods or materials from a foreign country for sale.

manioc a root crop like a potato or a yam, which originally grew in the Amazon but is now grown industrially. Also known as cassava.

pardos a word describing mixed-race Brazilian people with white, black and Indian ancestry.

Planalto a high plateau in the Centre-west region of Brazil.

plantation a large area where crops such as coffee or sugar cane are grown in orderly rows.

rainforest a forest that receives more than 1 m (3.3 ft) of rainfall spread evenly throughout the year.

republic a political system whose head of state is not a king or queen, but a president who has been elected by the people.

resources things that are available to use, often to help develop a country's industry and economy. Resources could be minerals, workers (labour) or water.

Sertão a large area of semi-desert in the North-east region of Brazil.

Further information

Books

Brazil (Destination Detectives)
by Ali Brownlie Bojang
(Raintree, 2007)

Countries of the World: Brazil
by Brian Dicks
(Evans Brothers, 2002)

Wealth of Nations: Brazil
by Jen Green
(Wayland, 2001)

The Changing Face of Brazil
by Edward Parker
(Wayland, 2007)

Travel Through: Brazil
by Joe Fullman
(QED Publishing, 2007)

Websites

**http://news.bbc.co.uk/1/hi/world/americas/
country_profiles/1227110.stm**
This is the BBC news page for Brazil, with recent
events and background information including a
timeline of major events.

**https://www.cia.gov/library/publications/
the-world-factbook/geos/br.html**
A good source of general statistics about Brazil.

http://www.brazil.org.uk
The Brazilian embassy in the UK.

http://www.saopaulo.sp.gov.br/
The website of the São Paulo State government.

http://www.governo.rj.gov.br
Information on Rio de Janeiro.

*Every effort has been made by the publisher to ensure
that these websites contain no inappropriate or offensive
material. However, because of the nature of the Internet,
it is impossible to guarantee that the contents of these sites
will not be altered. We strongly advise that Internet access
is supervised by a responsible adult.*

Index

Numbers in **bold** indicate pictures